WHY WAS I BORN?

WHY WAS I BORN?

Bridging Birth and Justice

....

by Dr. Richard Steinpach

GRAIL·FOUNDATION·PRESS

GAMBIER, OHIO

3rd revised edition

Cataloging-in-Publication Data
129
STE
Steinpach, Richard, 1917-1992
Why Was I Born? Bridging Birth and Justice : manuscript of a lecture by Richard Steinpach.—
Gambier, OH : Grail Foundation Press, ©1997.
102 p. ; 23 cm.
Includes bibliographies.
Summary: Applies the principles of eternal laws to the exploration and answering of fundamental questions, such as: Where did I come from?, Why am I here?, Where am I going, and How did I come to be the way that I am?.
ISBN 1-57461-013-9
1. Life - Origin 2. Reincarnation
3. Transmigration
129—dc20

Cover Photo: Jake Rajs
Cover Design and Typesetting: LM Design
Printer: Malloy Lithographing, Inc.

Printed on recycled paper.

Books by Dr. Richard Steinpach

FALSE WAYS
HOW CAN GOD ALLOW SUCH THINGS?
IT HAS BEEN DEMONSTRATED
THE LECTURES
"SEE THE TRUTH IS SO NEAR AT HAND..."
SELF-KNOWLEDGE
THE WAY AND THE GOAL
WHAT GOETHE WISHED TO TELL US
WHY WAS I BORN? BRIDGING BIRTH
AND JUSTICE
WHY WE LIVE AFTER DEATH

"We cannot live for ourselves alone. Our lives are connected by a thousand invisible threads, and along these sympathetic fibers, our actions run as causes and return to us as results."

–Herman Melville

This book contains the translation according to the sense of the original German text.
In some cases the words of the translation can only render the original meaning approximately.
Nevertheless, the reader will come to a good understanding if he or she absorbs inwardly the meaning of the contents.

What will you tell your child one day—and this is by no means so unusual—if he asks reproachfully, "Why did you bring me into this world? I certainly didn't ask you to!"

C O N T E N T S

....

FOREWORD   xv

INTRODUCTION *by Richard Anderson*   xvii

WHY WAS I BORN?   1

BIBLIOGRAPHY   55

ABOUT THE AUTHOR   57

APPENDIX A:

IN THE LIGHT OF THE TRUTH

THE GRAIL MESSAGE

An Introduction   59

APPENDIX B:

OTHER TITLES FROM

GRAIL FOUNDATION PRESS   67

....

. . . .

*B*etween 1979 and 1990, Richard
Steinpach gave hundreds of lectures on
various topics throughout the German-
speaking world. The powerful response
to his lectures not only confirmed the
relevance of the topics he discussed, but also compelled him
to publish them in book form. Grail Foundation Press is
pleased to publish Dr. Steinpach's works in America for
the first time.

. . . .

hy was I born?... is a seemingly simple question and yet the need to ask it may be symptomatic of the extent to which we have lost our way. Long ago we closed ourselves to the voice of the spirit, our true self, in the head-long pursuit of material things. As a result, our connection with the world beyond the physical has atrophied, and with it our ability to see the broader connections in life. In the process, we have become blind to, and therefore ignorant of, all reality that extends beyond the grasp of the physical senses.

...And why are we born into such vastly different circumstances? One is born into poverty, another into prosperity. One person enters the world with debilitating handicaps, while another is born in perfect health. A child comes to parents who love and nurture, another to parents who abuse. The list goes on and on. We see this disparity of circumstances around us every day. Sooner or later in the life of every individual, the question of justice invariably surfaces: Why are some given every advantage in life from the very outset while others seem to be constantly besieged by problems of every kind? Where is the justice? Where is the personal choice? Where is free will?

As the world catapults towards a new millennium, we find ourselves confronted with a perplexing array of challenges. On almost every front and in every field of endeavor exponential change portends both catastrophe *and renewal. We experience catastrophe when our vision is short-sighted, and we see only short-term solutions to our problems. But we are transformed and renewed when we live by the fundamental shifts in awareness emerging in science, education, medicine, and spirituality, where all aspects of life are seen as being interconnected, with the same laws operating uniformly throughout. What will this shift in thinking mean as it takes hold of the greater consciousness of humanity?...*

Indeed, we live in "the best of times and the worst of times."

Never before have more people enjoyed a standard of living that even the kings of old could not command. Everywhere we look, we see the material wealth created by a technical revolution that began 150 years ago, and has continued unabated since. Now, powerful technologies like personal computers and the Internet make an unheard of amount of information available to anyone who can "go on-line." Communication cycle times are decreasing at a geometric pace that results in a dramatically accelerated rate of change. We have no choice but to keep up and hang on or get left behind.

But where are we going? Where is this unprecedented change leading us, and what are we giving up in the process? In spite of our progress, we see disturbing signs of things gone awry. The nuclear family, once a part of larger, extended communities, is under attack from all sides. Many children are raised by day-care providers or others outside the home, and our youth too often find themselves without any hold on life because they have never experi-

enced a sense of belonging or of being needed. They look at the world around them and wonder where they fit in, if they fit in, and what if any purpose their lives could serve.

The problems in nuclear families manifest in society at large: drugs, teen pregnancy, single parents, gangs, the breakdown of the educational system, and the decay of many central cities. Our fascination with looking to the government to solve our problems has too often resulted in large, unwieldy bureaucracies that spend a large part of our income and commit each of us to a growing debt without addressing the underlying problems. In the world at large, we are continually exposed to a barrage of bad news from all sides: economies in a state of collapse, governments brutalizing their citizens, acts of genocide fomented by age-old ethnic animosities, and environmental catastrophes that expose increasing numbers of people to toxins, radiation, and unclean air and water.

Even "natural disasters" seem to have increased in keeping pace with accelerating change in the man-made world. Within the last few years, America alone has experienced enormous floods, extensive droughts, earthquakes, hurricanes and other disturbances of an intensity—and with a frequency—unmatched in our collective experience. We blame global warming, the ozone layer, and other man-made causes, but when really pressed, we must admit that we don't know what is driving the intensity of events both man-made and natural.

When faced with this startling array of problems, at both the micro and macro levels, basic survival instincts dictate one of two responses: escape or confrontation.

In an escape strategy, the senses are numbed so that nothing can get through to shock the psyche. One lives in a cocoon of his or her own fashioning, frequently rushing about, working endless hours, or in some cases becoming dependent on alcohol, drugs, television, or any number of other addictive behaviors. Such a person is not quite alive and not dead either, yet tries desperately, in all the wrong ways, to maintain some sense of equilibrium in a world out of kilter...

The other course is to open one's eyes wide in order to understand the nature of events pressing relentlessly forward towards an as yet unknown future. However, in spite of heroic attempts to understand, many of us find ourselves coming up short, for we have long since buried the key to understanding the world around us: understanding ourselves. Too many of us are born, live, and die without ever addressing the serious but simple questions of life: Where did I come from?, Why am I here?, and How did I come to be the way that I am? We have created a world in which it is all too easy to avoid such questions, even though, at some level of our being, the questions haunt us, begging to be answered.

Furthermore, we have created ways of thinking about the world—paradigms—that preclude at the outset any possibility for seeing the root causes of our problems or the essential nature of our being. For hundreds of years, we have pursued the thought that the universe and everything in it are here to serve man and that life on earth can ultimately be understood by knowing its most elemental parts.

We are now increasingly aware that this search for "basic building blocks" has proven futile and has yielded to a "quantum" view of the world wherein everything is interconnected. In this case physical reality is an illusion and only masks a deeper reality where radiation and energy are the form and substance of life. This new view, spearheaded by science, is shattering long-held paradigms of how the world works and is causing us to take another look at ourselves. It is as if someone has opened a window and allowed a fresh breeze to blow, one that offers new hope and a stirring of the spirit of man, long since ignored as superfluous.

And yet these new findings of science, and the resulting influx of thoughts regarding the nature of the world around us, are only hinting at a knowledge we have buried within us: that we are spiritual entities with a long history on this earth and the many planes that exist beyond physical reality. With this rediscovered knowledge we can begin the journey to understanding ourselves, and in doing so, at least start the work of correcting the endemic problems that plague us.

Dr. Richard Steinpach, in his book, Why Was I Born? Bridging Birth & Justice, *deals with the fundamental question, Who am I? In so doing, he gives the key to understanding ourselves and enables us to see far beyond that horizon dictated by our established view of the world. This book, together with his earlier publication,* Why We Live After Death, *casts a bright light on the previously enigmatic poles of human existence: birth and death. In the process, Steinpach creates a glimpse of life in perfect bal-*

ance, orchestrated by eternal laws that constantly return to each individual exactly that which has been personally woven on the great loom of creation. Steinpach offers the reader solid ground on which to stand in a world of shifting sands.

As we speed towards our destiny in a time of unprecedented change, we can choose between ignoring the warning signs of a world out of balance or we can resolve to find that quiet place within ourselves that offers true shelter from the storm. Richard Steinpach has written a book that directs us to that place.

Richard Anderson
Waterville, Ohio

WHY WAS I BORN?

*Manuscript of
a lecture by
Dr. Richard Steinpach*

*A*t the beginning of every earthlife is birth. This starting point of our pathway through life is determined initially by the environmental and social conditions into which we are born and by the abilities generally assumed to be inherited from our forefathers. But why do we set out with such unequal conditions? Would you or I even exist if our parents had each found other partners? In other words, is our existence simply a product of chance? Sooner or later, probably every thinking person asks himself why human births are fraught with so many inconsistencies.

What really do we know about the inception of human life? We believe we have a thorough grasp of it, since we are able, biologically speaking, to manipulate it. We can prevent conception and birth where they are not desired, and we can bring them about even where they would not normally be possible.

But it is with regard to test-tube fertilization, which has been extended to the point of surrogate mothers, that we find ourselves suddenly confronted by a host of insoluble genetic, legal and ethical problems. We do not really feel comfortable with this "progress"; on the other hand, the warning voices against abortion will not be silenced. A great many opposing views have been expressed about these issues in recent years, sufficient to shake our complacent self-assurance.

But first let me assure you that none of the arguments from either side will be repeated or added to here. The simple fact that even today we hold differing views about a process that has taken place in the same way since the beginning of mankind is indeed frightening evidence of how little we really know about the whole matter. We experiment with the existence of this creature "man" without being absolutely clear about what man actually is, and what purpose this earthlife really serves.

Therefore, I ask you: In the course of numerous dissertations and discussions have you ever received an answer to these questions? Or can it be that the answer is so obvious that there is no more to be said on the subject?

In 1970, the renowned biologist Ludwig von Bertalanffy gave one of his books the title ...*But of man we know nothing*, and as recently as 1984, the Salzburg Colloquium on Humanism considered the question: "What does medical science know of man?"

Our picture of man is still controversial, and the question remains: Is man this physical body? When discussing the concept, is it not striking that everyone will say that he *has* a body? How naturally we separate the body from the ego, making it a possession, not identical with our ego. In addition we also speak of a "soul." But what is this soul? What does the word "soul" bring to mind?

Let us now discuss this missing dimension. Only by so doing can we recognize the hidden connections behind the facade of outward appearances, a facade along which, to be honest, we proceed rather unsuspectingly and helplessly. For, unfortunately, a mystery still surrounds the coming-into-being of man. And this mystery is virtually unrelated to the physical side of our existence; rather it concerns all that actually determines our being human. Therefore, it is necessary to consider this "being human" from the *spiritual* point of view.

Of course I may be using a concept that for some of you is too vague, too meaningless and expressionless. If you ask someone, "What exactly is spirit?" that person will probably be surprised at first and then may reply, "The intellect, reason..." Hardly anyone will say, "It is I myself!" The essential human tradgedy lies in our inability to recognize the very nature of our own species. Man has lived on this planet for thousands of years, and yet still largely repudiates himself, since the intellectual game of fostering doubt is more important to him than the call from his inner being. Yet as long as man does not have clarity about himself, he lacks the starting point for all deliberations, for he cannot judge what is really of benefit to him, and what accords with the purpose of his existence.

Therefore, let it be made absolutely clear: our innermost core, our actual ego, is *spirit*. But do not confuse this concept with worldly cleverness, with the intellect. The intellect, which we so often take to be the spirit, is but a data bank for information, a calculating machine that can be imitated by a computer for purely earthly purposes. In sober, matter-of-fact thought processes, as in technology, the intellect is capable of notable achievements. But just as a computer is dependent upon the substance of the machine, the so-called hardware, so the intellect requires the material instrument of the brain. The spirit, however, is of a totally different, non-material species.

You may perhaps wish to say, "Well, that is just an assertion. Where is the proof?" May I say something fundamental to you about this? Only earthly things can be proved by material means, but never Truth, which transcends the boundaries of matter. I also want to tell you why this is so and can never be otherwise. By "proving," we mean investigating something with our senses: sight, hearing, smell, taste, and touch. These senses are all bound to our physical body, but the extra-sensory cannot be grasped through them any more than water can be drawn with a net. At best a few drops will cling to it. These drops may be likened, in connection with our subject, to the findings of para-psychology, where we learn that true understanding, genuine recognition, cannot be gained through the senses.

Only in spirit can you experience proof of the spirit. And here you will actually find it, for you bear it within yourself. In science there is the so-called "information theory," a rather high-sounding term for what is basically a very simple fact, e.g., that two liters cannot be poured into a one-liter container. Or, as expressed in different, more general terms, that nothing can reach beyond itself, beyond the boundaries set by its own species. However, you are actually able to grasp, to perceive intuitively and to experience love and hate, joy and sorrow, beauty, gratitude—in short, extra-material values. Here, in the sense of the "information theory," lies proof that you bear within you what is extra-material, since otherwise you would be unable to comprehend these values.

Even distinguished scientists are today no longer afraid of calling this spirit by name. Thus for example the brain research scientist, Nobel Prize-winner Sir John Eccles, writes in his book *The Self and Its Brain*, "As a neuronal machine the brain in principle cannot perform the necessary integration (this refers to the grasping of all those things that constitute our being human). An active and independent spirit, which makes use of the brain as an instrument, is needed for this." [1]

---

[1] Co-authored with Karl Popper

This insight precisely confirms what has all along been set forth in the book *In the Light of Truth: The Grail Message* by Abd-ru-shin. There it says:

"*We must at last learn to distinguish between the spirit and the intellect, the vital core of man and his tool!*"

This extra-material core, the spirit, is enveloped by several increasingly dense coverings. We know that material substance, which appears so solid to our senses, has issued from radiation, which becoming ever denser, suddenly enters our material world. Yet is material substance anything other than layers of coverings held together by the attraction power called "energy," which constitutes the core of every elementary particle? The basic principle involved is quite natural.

In this earthly world, don't we also wear coverings of varying density, depending on the conditions in which we find ourselves at the time—a shirt or a blouse, a suit or a dress, and finally an overcoat? And the less light and heat there is, the denser and heavier these coverings become. Therefore, the human spirit, far away from the radiant starting-point of Creation, also wears the densest covering, the physical body.

And this brings us to one of the most far-reaching causes of our lack of understanding: medical science is still primarily occupied with this "winter coat" of the spirit. Although conversant with the psycho-somatic concept — the interdependence between soul (psyche) and body (soma)—modern medicine only senses there is something that lies beyond the material. In the language of science this "something" is, as Arthur Koestler once mockingly put it, the "ghost in the machine," elusive because it cannot be grasped, and yet a reality existing behind the mechanical and chemical processes.

This "ghost in the machine," that cannot be grasped with material means, is the *spirit*. When it bears a covering of fine material substance the spirit can be called "soul" to differentiate it from the spirit itself. Hence soul—and here I am following the explanation given us in the book *In the Light of Truth*—is by no means something vague and indeterminate. It is the spirit in a covering of fine material substance. Since nature makes no leaps, and one step always follows another, the soul is connected with the physical body through a covering of denser material substance, the astral body. At the same time, the astral body acts as a bridge. Like a mold, it is, so to speak, the model for the physical body.

Now imagine these cloaks pushed into one another, like a telescope, and connected with each other through radiation. This connection has long since been verified by science. The elementary particles of which our material substance is composed are not mechanically connected, locked in position, or screwed together. Between them lie vast distances, bridged solely by radiation. Radiation holds the universe together, and each object radiates its own characteristic way. In fact, we can determine its condition from the nature of this radiation. What we regard as color is the reflected radiation of light. Invisible heat radiation can be captured through infra-red photography. We make the radiation of our vital processes "visible" in the form of brain currents. During sleep, brain current activity is decisively reduced, and at death this radiation ceases altogether, thus indicating that the holding fast of the soul, its connection with the physical body, is associated with this radiation, and is dependent upon it.

For the purpose of this lecture I do not wish to enlarge on this topic, but have gone into the subject at great length in another lecture entitled *Why We Live After Death* (Grail Foundation Press, 1995).

Therefore I would like to conclude this portion of the discussion with a sentence from the famous physicist Max Planck, who openly acknowledged his realization: "The actual, the real, the true, is not visible and transient material substance, but the invisible, immortal spirit."

Finally, I would ask all who are not yet satisfied with these inevitably brief references to admit the existence of the spirit as a working hypothesis—at least for the time being—in order to understand what follows.

Now you will probably want to ask: If our innermost core is spirit and if spirit is something extra-material, for what purpose are we actually here on earth in material substance? This question too, requires an answer if we are to concern ourselves with the birth of man. For surely the process is meaningless if we cannot say what purpose is really served by human existence. Therefore we must deal with this question first.

What will you tell your child one day—and this is by no means so unusual—if he asks reproachfully, "Why did you bring me into this world? I certainly didn't ask you to!"

The answer is very simple: development. Every earth life is nothing but an opportunity for this, an opportunity for the further development of each individual human spirit.

Let us look at the history of this planet. It took millions of years for this material world to condense out of cosmic nebulae, allowing those compounds, which initially became the foundation of plant life, to arise from the primeval element hydrogen. And plant life gradually evolved from the simplest, least demanding form—from lichens, mosses and algae—to the point where it could offer the basis of existence to animal life. This animal life too, starting with the simplest organisms in the primeval water of the sea, over long periods of time and through the evolutionary stages of fish and amphibian finally conquered the land. Everything lay in the radiation of the Creator-Power, the Primordial Energy, in readiness for its subsequent form.

Note, however, this very important aspect: each form could only be "called forth" gradually when in each case, the precondition was created, through similarity, for the connection with the next higher form.

The human form is characteristic of the human spirit. More specifically, the spirit shapes its covering, both ethereal and astral, in the manner familiar to us as the physical body. Therefore to enable the human spirit to gain a foothold here on this earth, that body form most nearly approaching the human body had to be brought to the highest possible degree of perfection. This form was the body of the anthropoid ape. Only then could the inert, unawakened *human spirit*, still awaiting its development, appear as something *completely new* in the material world. Wherever the human spirit entered such an animal body it effected the further development of the form into that of a human being. From then on the ways parted and man's own path of development began. This was—of course not only in a single creature—the origin of man on earth.

Note the crucial precondition for the incarnation of the spirit. The vessel, the material form, had to mature towards the spirit, so to speak, in order to receive it. I especially emphasize this point because we shall subsequently encounter the same requirement. This joining of what is relatively similar—on the one hand the most highly developed animal form nearest to man, on the other, the still-undeveloped human spirit—is what obscures the boundary because the new does not yet stand out enough. And for this reason science is also hardly in a position to classify the various discoveries of bones and state categorically which is still animal and which was already man.

Hence the Darwinian theory of the origin of the species is both right and wrong. The theory is correct with regard to the body covering, but it overlooks the completely *new motivating impetus to further development* added by the spirit. The assertion that man has descended from the ape is like the contention that the automobile descended from the horse-drawn cart because they both have wheels and are means of transportation. We would smile at such a statement since we know that the engine makes all the difference and that this completely dissimilar kind of motive power facilitates performance that no horse-drawn vehicle could achieve. And just as the automobile has developed from the first slowly chugging vehicle up to the modern fast racing car, so too the human spirit has continued to develop from its early forms to that being who has achieved all that is summed up in the concept "culture," which represents the true accomplishments of the spirit.

With each birth this evolutionary history of the species is repeated in rapid tempo. The embryo develops hints of gills, then an amphibious tail, and finally a fur covering, undergoing once more in condensed form, the material-animal sequence of evolution and mankind's early stages of consciousness that once required hundreds of thousands of years. The slow process of orientation in the earthly world is today compressed into childhood. And even this childhood is becoming shorter and shorter as the young mature ever earlier. Although we build upon the preceding development, the latitude available to us for the continuation of this development expands steadily, so that we can add new aspects to the process. There is an acceleration, a certain urgency in this happening. And this acceleration is significant!

But of what does this development consist? We are in the habit of saying apologetically, "Nobody is perfect," and with that we hit exactly upon the right thing. For man from his earliest beginnings is and remains a learner. He is by no means fully conscious of his abilities, his possibilities, and requirements, since the human spirit initially is only a *spirit-germ*. Like the shoot of a plant, each spirit needs external influences to develop the talents resting within it. For the plant it is soil, sun, wind and weather that further its growth; for man it is joy and sorrow—in short, it is *experience* that helps him to mature. Just as physically we could not place one foot in front of the other if there were no friction, so too, in order to advance, the spirit needs "friction" with the environment—that is, contact and coming-to-terms with it.

"Life learns from itself—through continuous feedback." This is how biologist Professor Rupert Riedl outlines the essence of evolution. And this process is certainly not over yet; each man continues for himself, for his spirit. The ongoing development of spiritual talents is indeed nothing but the continuation of what we have recognized in material substance as "evolution," namely the bringing forth of increasingly mature manifestations. And the very process of learning that lay at the root of this development, the ever-improving adaptation to the realities of the environment enforced by the reciprocal action and determined by the Laws of Nature, is also the means to spiritual progress. Experiencing is the "feedback" that brings man the answer to his volition and deed, and thereby helps him to maturing realization. The ancient folk wisdom "practice is better than theory" expresses this precisely. The accumulation of knowledge acquired by lifeless study is of no benefit to the spirit. Only experience that has been assimilated and filled with life through reciprocal action has value.

And now let us consider an example: What happens when an apprentice joins a firm? How does his training proceed? He will first become acquainted with his immediate sphere of activity; he will have to begin by training and developing his abilities to be able to use them effectively. Gradually he will learn also to understand the interaction among the departments and discover the significance of his activity within the framework of the whole.

If he then wishes to grow into ever higher tasks, he will have to pay attention to the economic rules and regulations and learn that only those products of use to the buyer will find a market. The understanding that arises from this learning is simply that his own profit depends on the benefit he provides for others through his activity.

All this seems rather obvious to us. But note here how much we follow—indeed, must follow—the rules that govern our own course of development. For the Laws of Creation remain ever the same, in great things as well as in small. The laws merely manifest in the various spheres of activity in a way that is characteristic of these spheres.

Like apprentices, we human spirits, at one time, began our development. Now we have reached the stage where we know how to make use of some of our abilities—not always very skillfully either. We still lack understanding of the connections, of how to fit our activities into the great, complete whole. This shortcoming applies not only to earthly things, where today's ecological problems demonstrate quite clearly to us this lack of understanding, but to a far greater extent with regard to our place and task in Creation.

Man, the apprentice, often acts like an immature youth who, instead of concerning himself with the far-away goal of his ascent, leads a carefree existence with only his comfort, his well-being, and his pleasures in mind. That is precisely what we do when we put our extremely short-term imaginary advantages in the first place and do not ask what will benefit our spiritual development.

We should long since have become conscious of what we have to learn. Our task is to recognize the Laws of this Creation, in which we are a cooperating part because of the influence we exert. It is no longer necessary for the religions to remind us of our responsibility; the natural sciences already see to that. For example, the well-known science journalist Hoimar von Ditfurth writes: "One of the most exciting results of modern science is the fact that from the vast number of individual results produced by it there begins to emerge more clearly, as though fitted together from countless mosaic pieces, the picture of a world in which everything is interconnected, the greatest with the smallest, the nearest with the furthest....A united, integrated world." (*Wir sind nicht nur von dieser Welt [We are not only of this World]*, Hoffman and Campe/Hamburg)

The prominent biochemist and environmentalist Frederic Vester actually completes this thought with the words, "When all at once it was established that every system projects into another, that not a single one exhausts itself in its own sphere of life, it became clear that here too there could be no separate rules." (*Neuland des Denkens* DVA *Breaking New Ground for Thought.*

Consider the full significance of this statement! There can be no separate rules! Everything is subject to the same laws! Man is no exception either!

The latest scientific findings, within their limitations, confirm what was stated long ago in *In the Light of Truth*:

"*There always rests in everything only the same simple Law! In the finest spiritual as in the coarsest earthly. Without change and without deviation. It takes effect and must be observed.*"

We must adjust to this lawfulness, for the Law forms the framework of our existence. And since we as spiritual creatures are capable of and destined for conscious activity, this adjusting must also be achieved consciously—that is, knowingly. With the plant and the animal, evolution, as we have discovered, has always ensured that whatever did not adapt to its living conditions died out, was eliminated, became extinct. How can we assume that it would be any different with us? This insight is slowly beginning to dawn on us in connection with manifold environmental problems.

In our small daily affairs we have long been practicing these realizations. What would you tell your young son if he failed to solve his mathematics problem correctly, for instance if he calculated 3x3=8? However much he pleads and begs, "Dad, I really tried to do everything right; please let 3x3=8!" you will nevertheless have to say to him, "My dear child, I am sorry, but there is no haggling or quibbling. The laws of mathematics are simply immovable. You will just have to do the example again, for your work has to be practiced until you get it right!"

If you, as a responsible parent with your child's progress at heart, were to speak as such, you would, strictly speaking, have thereby acknowledged and put into practice two perceptions that are of vast importance for your whole existence. First, you have established that there are rules that are immovable, before which there can be only "right" or "wrong." And this applies specifically to the Laws of Creation, for which mathematics is simply a means of making these Laws comprehensible.

And secondly, in demanding that the wrongly-solved problem be repeated, you have recognized the purpose of rebirth and reincarnation, which is still a mystery to many people. Moreover you have realized the need for it! For rebirth is indeed the grace that allows us to atone for mistakes made and to go on learning, since the subject matter that we are permitted to assimilate can as little be grasped in one life as your son would have exhausted the whole field of mathematics if he had rightly calculated 3x3=9. You see, this is why so many people cling to life on earth, thinking that there is still so much to be put to use and experienced. They quite correctly perceive intuitively the magnitude of the task yet to be mastered.

Reincarnation makes it possible for us to continue this learning process. But just as a pupil must finally be rejected if he fails to reach the required standard, despite all the re-examinations offered him, so too is the possibility for our spiritual development (which must first take place here in the dense World of Matter) limited by the ripeness of this planet. Astrophysics recognized only a few decades ago what we have long since been told in the work *In the Light of Truth:* that each heavenly body passes through a cycle of development and dissolution.

However, we should not imagine that this end lies in the unforeseeable future. Consider that millions of years passed before man could become established on this earth. Accepting the scientific assertions that our central star, the sun, will one day explode into a red giant and finally implode in a gravitational collapse, we can easily imagine that long before that time human life, which is bound to very definite and narrowly limited conditions, will no longer be possible on this planet. Moreover, man's behavior is even zealously directed toward rendering the planet uninhabitable long before that. You can therefore realize the obvious limitation set on the possibility of spiritual development even in the course of rebirths. For by then the spirit already must have had all the experiences it can have only in material substance and that are required for its maturing. Through these experiences it must have so grown in strength—that is, become conscious of its possibilities and tasks within the framework of Creation—that it can now exist as spirit in the extra-material worlds without the support of material substance. This is the selfsame Law, but obviously in much greater dimension, that we can observe in the earthly world. The child too, on attaining adulthood, must be able to do without parental care if he is not to become unfit for life. Also, the fruit must fall from the tree after its ripening, otherwise it will decay.

Perhaps you may still think: "Reincarnation—again, that is only conjecture! Wouldn't I know something about it if I have lived a number of times before?" This argument, frequently advanced to refute reincarnation, has long been invalidated by science. We know today that everything we retain in our memory for more than about twenty minutes, the so-called "long-term memory," comes into being through the forming and storing of protein compounds in the brain. But this brain, like the whole body, decays after earthly death. With rebirth we receive a new body and with it a new brain, in whose day-conscious memory there cannot logically exist those protein compounds that were once formed in another brain. This new brain is like an unrecorded magnetic tape. If you buy such a new, unrecorded cassette, you do not expect to discover on the tape a recording you made previously on another. Therefore, the experiences and the lessons of former existences cannot be found in our day-conscious memory; they have entered into our spirit, into our personality. They determine the character, the abilities, and the talents that we bring with us at birth, as the formative result of our previous journeys through existence. And at times some faint memory of past lives flashes in the spirit as a "deja vu" experience that we cannot associate with the present earthly life.

Consider the very fact that past-life memories are generally hidden from us as a grace that enables us—unburdened with conscious recognition from the past—to confront those situations and persons with whom we may be linked by ill-fated entanglements from previous lives. Redemption is thereby made easier for us.

In this connection let me immediately address a second argument that is always cited against reincarnation: How is it that formerly so few and now so many people live on earth? Where have all these human spirits come from if they are supposed to have lived several times before? This answer is also quite simple. Take a certain quantity and divide it into two parts, as you like. The total quantity always remains the same, no matter the amount that may be in one part or the other. Therefore we must not consider only the one side, namely our earthly world; the other side, the beyond, must be included. Of the total number of human spirits seeking to achieve maturity on earth—which comprises those on this side as well as in the beyond—more and more are now being incarnated here simultaneuosly. In view of the advanced state of the earth, so many spirits are in need of this opportunity for subsequent maturing.

To more than half of mankind on our globe—to all of the Far East—reincarnation, even if to some extent in slightly distorted conceptions, is a foregone conclusion. Only we in the West feel constrained to doubt it. But we do so against all reason. Don't we see the alternation in all the rhythms of nature (summer and winter, day and night, ebb and flow, offshore and onshore winds, development and decay, blossom and fruit, fruit and seed)? Always one thing calls forth the other. We too bear this law within us: breathing in compels us to breathe out, breathing out compels us to breathe in. Every beat of our heart pumps out blood and sucks it back; the blood circulates continuously from the systemic to the pulmonary side, back and forth, the sides constantly interchanging. And all these manifestations trace the form of a wave, termed mathematically "the sine curve," forming alternately an upward and a downward arc. Wherever this arc intersects the straight line of the zero-axis, the crossover point represents a change from one side to the other and vice versa.

Birth and death are merely such crossover points in the rhythm of human existence. Birth into earth-life is death in the beyond and earthly death is birth on the other side.

If, despite my earlier point about the limited value of earthly proofs in these matters, you should still want proof, may I suggest that you ask those who deny rebirth! Supporting those who are convinced about rebirth is the logic of the Laws of Life; let the others attempt to prove that just here life acts *contrary* to the universally valid Laws. Such proof can never be given because these Laws are adamantine and uniform.

Reincarnation has also been compatible with Christianity from the very beginning—a surprising fact to many. We read in the New Testament how at that time people variously assumed John the Baptist and Jesus to be the prophet Elijah reborn. But Elijah lived in the 9th century before Christ. The Evangelists also report that the people spoke of a rebirth of the prophet Jeremiah. The latter, however, lived in the 7th century before Christ. Jesus certainly rejected these assumptions with regard to His person, but not by any means the idea of rebirth. On the contrary, the Evangelist Matthew even believed that Jesus confirmed John the Baptist to have been Elijah reborn (Matthew 11: 11-14 and 17: 10-13).

And in John 9:1-3 we read, "And as Jesus passed by, he saw a man blind from birth. And his disciples asked Him, saying, 'Master, who did sin, this man, or his parents, that he was born blind?'"

How can someone have sinned before his birth? The question asked by the disciples certainly points, not necessarily in doubt but as a possible cause, to guilt from a *former* life and therefore logically to that life itself. The question is based on the knowledge of reincarnation and the fateful connections ensuing from a previous life. And how does Jesus react? Shouldn't he have rejected this question because of its absurdity? Shouldn't he perhaps have said, "How could you think of such a thing?" But nothing of the kind happens. Jesus gives an objective reply, containing both alternatives: "Neither hath this man sinned, nor his parents: but that the works of God should be made manifest in him," thus referring to the healing of the blind man, which took place afterward.

As is well known, the Gospels were written long after the death of Jesus. Yet it was not considered necessary to omit these clear references to reincarnation, to express them differently, or at least to explain them. Surely this proves that the knowledge of reincarnation survived well after the time of Jesus.

In fact, in the theology of Origen, who, and I quote here from an encyclopedia, "was the greatest scholar and by far the most prolific theological writer of this time and moreover of the whole church before Augustine," we also find the idea of the correlation and interdependence of several lives.

The knowledge of reincarnation is essential to being able to grasp our human existence as a complete whole. Without it we fare as one who would judge the action of a play, a film, or a novel on the basis of a single scene or chapter. We are bound to come to wrong conclusions because we lack the knowledge of the connections.

Hence we read from *In the Light of Truth: The Grail Message:*

"*But one of the chief mistakes so many people make is that they judge only according to gross matter, regarding themselves as the center in it, and taking into consideration one earth-life, whereas in reality they already have several earth-lives behind them. These, as well as the intervening times in the Ethereal World, are equal to one uniform existence, through which the threads are tightly stretched without breaking, so that in the effects of a particular earthly existence only a small part of these threads therefore becomes visible.*

"Hence it is a great mistake to believe that at birth an absolutely new life begins, that a child is thus 'innocent,' and that all happenings can be accounted for in only the short life on earth. If this were true, then the existing Justice would naturally require the combined causes, effects and reactions to take place within the span of one earth-life.

"Turn away from this error. You will then soon discover in everything that happens the logic and justice which at present are so often missed!"

From this we must now come to the conclusion that we have all lived repeatedly on earth before! And because of the advanced ripeness of this celestial body, it has been a long time since anyone was born here for the first time.

We must ask ourselves, then, how it could happen that the knowledge of reincarnation, which evidently existed in early Christianity, has been lost? To this end let me recount some historical facts, which unfortunately are far too little known.

Long after the death of Origen, the Christian world was convulsed by severe conflicts. These concerned above all the question of whether Jesus had been God-man in *one* person or God *and* man, thus uniting *two* natures within Himself. Although it may seem incomprehensible to us today that people could presume to decide upon such a question, yet at that time this conflict of opinion—in connection with the interpretation given by council resolutions later recorded in history as the so-called "Three Chapters Controversy"—shook the political unity of the Roman Empire. The long-deceased Origen had, in his writings, supported the monophysitic doctrine, the concept of the one-fold nature of Jesus, which was fiercely opposed by the so-called Diophysites, the believers in the two-fold nature. As a result of these conflicts, some provinces were ultimately even threatening to secede. For this reason the Emperor Justinian I convoked an Ecumenical Council, which finally met in Constantinople in 553. The Emperor sought to offer each of the opposing parties a favorable outcome by means of a two-fold decision. To satisfy the Diophysites, Origen, since he was cited by the Monophysites, would be anathematized as a heretic and his teaching rejected. In return the Monophysites, through a decision agreeable to them in the "Three Chapters Controversy," would emerge as victors.

To this end *the Emperor*, as the self-proclaimed highest ecclesiastical authority (it was the age of the most pronounced imperial papalism, which combined secular and ecclesiastical power) *himself* dictated the resolutions to be passed by the Ecumenical Council, including the one anathematizing the entire works of Origen. The Pope, Vigilius I, refused for more than six months to sign the resolutions of the Council and thereby make them binding on the whole church. As a result he was detained in Constantinople by the Emperor and only allowed to leave the city after he had more or less agreed with the Council's resolutions in two letters addressed to the Emperor.

I have related this in detail because, to me, it concerns one of the greatest tragedies in western spiritual history. Here *a decision on a matter of faith* of the greatest significance was *enforced* by *secular* authority solely out of political expediency. Through the total condemnation of Origen's works—unrelated to the question of reincarnation—reference to a succession of lives, mutually conditioned by the basic Laws of Cause, Effect, and Reaction[2], was eliminated from the treasures of the Christian faith.

Thus we drag with us like a spiritual shackle the legacy of Justinian and his time, for the denial of reincarnation has cut man off from the knowledge of the great meshwork of his existence. It makes us question the continuance of our ego, the outliving of our physical existence; it conceals from us the purpose of life and makes us doubt the justice of God. If we think of *this* birth as the origin of life, must it not seem unjust that one is born rich, another poor, one healthy, another sickly? Even the scientists stand perplexed before the question of why human beings are so indisputably different. The assumption that environmental factors are decisive for this has proved to be right only in certain conditions. Above all, research on the phenomenon of twins, especially identical twins who grew up apart in quite different circumstances, has all too clearly refuted such a view. The similar nature of such people, down to the last details of their behavior, idiosyncrasies, and interests, has pointed to a similarity in natural inclinations from birth. Should heredity be decisive? In that case, however, our personality would then be all the more a product of chance, of arbitrariness. Hence this world, which is undeniably controlled by lawful principles (consider for

---

[2] In our present or past lives we have by thought, word, or deed induced all that we are now experiencing. Fortified by everything of a like nature, the *effects* we have brought about constitute the natural *reactions* to what we ourselves once gave *cause*.

instance the statement of Nobel prize-winner Manfred Eigen: "The *oneness* of Nature manifests in its *Laws*.") would confront us from the very beginning with meaningless injustice, were we to take as a basis this *single* earth-life!

With the knowledge of reincarnation, man held the key to all these questions in his hands long ago, but heedlessly threw it away. It is high time for us to rediscover this key at last!

Of course some people simply shy away from concerning themselves with the idea of reincarnation because they fear the responsibility connected with it. If everything ends with earthly death, many things must remain unatoned. If, however, there is an afterlife and rebirth, the circumstances of our next life will of course be shaped by the good qualities we bring with us and also by our faults and weaknesses—all those ties clinging to us from former earth-lives that are yet to be severed. This responsibility frightens many people. Yet the Laws of Creation will not change, whether or not we wish to acknowledge them. It is therefore all the more necessary to face the facts and adjust our behavior accordingly.

Rebirth serves to illustrate how strongly the human spirit strives toward ever faster, ever richer development, provided it has passed beyond the primitive stage. Through the medium of communication the possibility of experiencing has grown from generation to generation as if by leaps and bounds. What utter injustice there would be in the differing lives of former earth-dwellers and those of the present, had we not all lived through these earlier stages as well!

But this multiplicity of things assailing us demands an ever greater activity of the spirit. It is not merely a question of assimilating the wealth of experience intellectually, nor certainly of being crushed by it. What matters is to gain recognition of the working of the Eternal Laws that sustain and permeate this Creation, taking effect in all happenings, and thereby becoming discernible to us. Unaffected by the changeable views of man, the *immovable Will of God* manifests in these Laws. It is this Will we must understand in order to advance spiritually.

Much of what I have explained so far may not seem to be directly concerned with the *birth* of man suggested by the lecture title. But with good reason we are told in the book *In the Light of Truth:*

"*You* must *lift your eyes* beyond *this earth, and recognize where your path leads after this earthly life, so that at the same time you may become aware of why and for what purpose you are here on this earth.*"

Thus I hope you will understand that until we could recognize the full significance of our *being man,* a significance by no means limited to this one earth-life, we were unable to deal in the right sense with man's *coming-into-being.* Only now are we in a position to fit the process into the wider context in which it belongs.

Now we stand before the fact that there is in reality no "human being;" there are only men and women, a fact that plays a very significant part in conception and birth. Although people today think that the sexes can be standardized, we cannot overlook their differing tasks. One hears with increasing frequency that the different spheres of interest are merely an "inculcated behavior in a particular role." Give the train set to the girl, the doll's kitchen to the boy, and specifically sex-linked inclinations would disappear. This belief expresses an alarming human arrogance, which, ignorant of the ordained purpose of each sex, presumptuously attempts to change the realities of Creation.

For the difference between the sexes is not only concerned with their role in the reproductive process; it is rooted in the spirit. This difference involves an order of gradation, which testifying to the Wisdom and Love of the Creator, serves as a kind of "development aid" for the human spirit.

Man's field of activity is coarser, more down-to-earth. He is more closely bound up with the earth than is woman. In the greater robustness of his body he also has the appropriate equipment for this activity. Woman's work, on the other hand, lies in caring, tending; it is closer to nature. It is determined by finer sensitivity, which is manifested in her physical structure. Such qualities as grace and charm are reserved to the womanly. Thus woman, whose nature is rooted in the spirit, forms the bridge to a finer world; she stands a little nearer to this less compact world than does the man. Through this situation alone, it is her task, quite unconsciously, to keep alive in him—who is closer to the earth—the longing for higher things.

Through her nature, woman can become an incentive for man to refine and ennoble himself. The very presence of a true woman is often able to bring this about. It is with good reason that Goethe says in *Tasso*, "And if you would know what is seemly, ask of noble women!"

Man quite rightly senses that it is his allotted task to protect the noble or true woman, who has preserved her womanly nature, from the hardships of this coarse world. This task can move man joyfully to unfold his highest virtues—thus consideration, chivalry and manly courage. This is the basis for the wrongly-understood disparaging concept of woman as the "weaker sex." Yet seen from the spiritual it is just in this somewhat looser connection with coarsest matter that the furthering power, the strength of woman, lies. Naturally it is strength of a different kind from that of man.

For this reason it is utterly wrong when the equal rights movement, which unfortunately has become necessary in our modern world, is directed towards opening up masculine fields of activity for women. Undoubtedly she is able to fill these positions, but often only by repressing her singular womanly characteristics and above all at the cost of over-straining herself, since she is usually not spared the womanly tasks of caring for home and children. Therefore we are going in exactly the wrong direction when we use masculine activity as the measure for the "raising" of woman's status instead of offering equal respect to the very different nature of woman's work.

In considering how to achieve this respect, we cannot use the present economic and social order as a basis. This order is the result of erroneous human attitudes. From the spiritual perspective, things can only be described as they *should* be, according to the Will of the *Creator*.

Therefore I have had to bring again to your awareness the lofty task which, in accordance with the Creation-plan, is allotted to woman for the spiritual upliftment of mankind. This bridge upwards into the finer, less material, given to humanity in the form of woman, serves not only to ennoble man, but also to provide the entry for new human life.

In the misunderstanding, denying, indeed withdrawing from the task of woman—all of which we can frequently observe—lies the real cause of many difficulties in relationships between partners and also in conception and birth.

I would remind you of my previous statement that everything in Creation is based on radiation. We read from *In the Light of Truth:*

"*For there is life only in radiation, and only in and through radiation is movement generated.*"

I ask you to consider the effects of this one statement, unrefuted by science, from which follows a conclusion of decisive importance for conception and birth. For only across the refined *radiation bridge* formed by the female spirit can a human spirit meant for embodiment reach this earthly world. Coming from the world beyond, a less dense world, the spirit needs this kind of radiation transition. Remember that everything forms as it becomes denser, coming from above, from the lighter and finer.

Therefore looking at things differently—from the spiritual point of view—the fact that only woman possesses the organs that support the development of another human body, is the material manifestation, the consequence of her mediator role, which is based on the feminine spiritual nature. Of no less importance is the radiation bridge thus formed. If the bridge is weakened or even destroyed by the woman becoming masculine, thus by an incisive change in her nature, then difficult pregnancies, premature births and even infertility may result. The cause of such complaints can certainly lie even in the spiritual. Not without ill effect can man alter what has been ordained by the Wisdom of God. Therefore it will never be possible to produce human life in the test-tube. The radiation of the feminine is needed. Even the so-called "test-tube babies" have had to be carried to full term by a woman after fertilization in the test-tube.

Only when it becomes clear to us that the sexual is rooted in the spiritual do we approach the significance of the generative power. The idea that it should or indeed may serve only the purpose of procreation belittles the generative power to something gross material and functional. This power is of much greater importance to the spirit.

During the years of childhood, when the physical body is maturing, the spirit lives sheltered as though behind a rampart. The instrument that it may use in this life is not yet developed. This means, expanding upon the statement about radiations cited earlier, that the spirit's radiation does not yet encompass the complete radiation-spectrum of this earthly world, is not yet fully open to it, and therefore cannot yet completely link up with it. The child is predominantly inclined to the world of nature as he lives through the early developmental stages of mankind. He bears no responsibility yet for earthly events. Our legal system expresses this quite correctly: the child is considered "under age," a minor. Others must act on his behalf. Only when he has come of age does he have his own ability to act, thus also full responsibility. What has taken place? Sexual maturity has set in, and as can be seen, has a very practical meaning. It is as though a drawbridge had been lowered, over which the spirit only now can truly connect with the outside world. Now responsible for its actions, the individual steps out into the world, but is also exposed to worldly influences. The actual significance of the generative power is that it provides the spirit with this full reciprocal interconnection with the earthly world. This power is the most mature expression of which the material body is capable. It is the vital energy of the adult human being on earth. We make use of it in everything we do, not only in sexual activity.

If now man and woman—the two parts of the creature "man," which though different are called to complementary activity—strive towards and are attracted to each other like opposite poles in physics, then the spiritual bond of love should establish the connection between them. One feels almost ashamed of having to emphasize something so self-evident, but our modern age has turned things upside down and placed the material, carnally-driven instinct "sex" in the forefront, the very opposite of love, which comes from the spirit. Reaching far beyond liking and harmony, love's significance is in the spiritual advancement of each partner. This alone enables the relationship between the partners to fulfill its true, higher purpose. Love indeed offers the strongest aid to spiritual ascent. Without compulsion it makes us exercise consideration and selflessness, disregarding our own ego for the benefit of the other. Through love a voluntary, joyful volition to serve comes alive. With that volition man grows into his task in Creation, learns to adapt him-

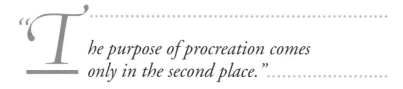

self in the fullest sense, and recognizes that only in giving can there also be receiving.

Only then does this love, meant for the other's spirit, for his whole being, seek to find its release through the body, because this body is simply the outer shell, the vessel of the beloved spirit. Then nothing unclean, nothing immoral, attaches to this expression. It can never be wrong to use the gift bestowed by the Creator in a natural way since it makes possible something that serves to create a gladdening complement between the partners: the exchange of ethereal fluid forces. Therefore we find in the work *In the Light of Truth* this sentence, so immensely important for understanding the generative power:

> "*The purpose of procreation comes only in the second place.*"

Now it may be that two partners who are so united "wish for a child" or "want to have a child." Notice how much these common expressions refer to the parents. This emphasis reflects our radically wrong attitude to the question of descendants. If a child gets lost somewhere in a crowd, the question "To whom does the child belong?" will almost certainly be asked. Yet the child does not "belong" to anyone—only to himself. He is not acquired like a piece of property. He is no toy. He is an independent human spirit, who just like his parents, has already journeyed through many lives. What distinguishes him from his parents is simply that his physical body must first be trained and educated, and as previously explained, that only at a certain stage of maturity of this body can his spirit work fully in an outward direction.

Anyone who sees in the child an employee or a provider—and already has plans for him at an early age—will and should be disappointed. The child has to tread *his own* path of spiritual development. He must experience what benefits *him*, not his parents. Every disregard of this principle would be a transgression of the Fifth Commandment. Let us not blind ourselves by imagining that killing relates only to the physical. That distinction is not written anywhere. From the spiritual standpoint—and it is from here that our existence is to be examined—every obstacle placed in the way of another's spiritual development, every suppression of his legitimate possibilities to evolve, is a killing.

In the Light of Truth explains what should be the true basis of the wish for a child. Pay strict attention to every word, since extremely important things are contained in these few sentences. They read as follows:

"*For spiritually free human beings procreation should be nothing but the proof of their willingness to take a strange human spirit into the family as a permanent guest, offering it the opportunity to atone and to mature on earth. Only when both sides have the fervent wish to* achieve this purpose *should the opportunity for procreation be sought.*"

Doesn't this happening now take on a completely different and much greater dimension? From this perspective we can gain a new understanding of the procreative ability that has been granted us. These words clarify the spiritual significance of conception and birth. There is no longer room for the selfish wishes of parents who "want to have a child." Instead we see the wonderful power of helpful love in service to another human spirit. An all-embracing Commandment of Creation can be realized: to love one's neighbor as oneself, to make possible for him what each of us should strive for as our own highest goal—to advance on the road to spiritual maturity!

Reciprocally, this striving will also result in spiritual gain for the parents. The trouble, the care they take over the child and the joy it gives them, all provide intense experiencing and make it possible for them to sever many, perhaps very old, entanglements. For the "strange" guest mentioned earlier is usually not so strange. The child's coming to just these parents does not take place arbitrarily but is on the basis of wise Laws. Becoming aware of the significance of conception and birth to both parents and child is fundamental for solving all further questions related to these processes in accord with the Laws of Creation.

While one woman may regard a child as unwanted and may do everything to prevent a pregnancy, another may take the opposite position. Her whole life, as we say, "is entirely devoted to motherhood." In it, she sees her highest goal, her fulfillment. This view is also wrong, for it is too limited. Motherhood is the noblest flower of the natural, "animistic," qualities of woman. The maternal in itself is also characteristic of female animals, but is not reserved solely for the human woman since motherhood also includes the spiritual significance of human development and is thus also of spiritual benefit to the mother. Indeed there is a gradation order in all this. Generative power is the most mature expression of the physical body, while motherhood is the noblest form of activity of the feminine nature. The two aspects, building upon each other, prepare the earthly foundation for the entry of the *spirit*. And since the spirit stands above these material manifestations, the mother must tread *her own* spiritual path. She is on earth for that purpose. She must see in motherhood only a lofty possibility toward achieving spiritual maturity. Motherhood is not the goal itself, not the purpose of her life.

The words of *In the Light of Truth* cited earlier state that procreation should take place only where the wish to welcome a new spirit exists on *both* sides. This means that in regard to this question human beings not only may, but even *must* make a decision; indeed procreation demands a harmonious decision of will on the part of both parents. For the coming-into-being of man is far too important an event to be made independent of man's spiritual volition. It is a question of *consciously* assuming responsibility for the benefit of an as-yet-unknown other. How much harm, what mental anguish has resulted from the denial of this freedom to decide—a freedom which should be self-evident by virtue of human dignity alone!

Of course at the same time we must note that our will is not always done, sometimes out of higher necessity. The words of *In the Light of Truth* quoted above refer to the "spiritually free" human being. This means only the one

36

whose will is not already bound through outstanding reactions from former decisions of will. Therefore only that human being who lives in accordance with the Laws of God is truly free. Wherever he does something that violates the Laws of Nature—in short something unnatural—he will incur consequences, and with them ties. This principle of reaction (called "reciprocal action"), which holds good in everything, has now been recognized by scientists as a Law of Nature. Every human being, because of his journeys in former lives, experiences such reactions from past wrong decisions. Because of these existing ties, things he does not like, that he seeks to avoid, have to occur periodically. This never happens to our detriment. What takes place is always only what benefits us spiritually, what helps us to sever existing entanglements and thereby to mature. But owing to our limited vision we are seldom able to perceive these connections.

Therefore even if we can make decisions about birth control (indeed we are meant to do so, since every decision is a small part of the process of maturing) the realization of these decisions must remain within the Laws of God. So you see many possibilities available to man today—by which he believes he can become free of obligations, efforts and cares—imply fateful ties for the future. These ties will always result when he acts against Nature. To understand this concept properly, use as a guiding principle this sentence from *In the Light of Truth*:

"*To be natural means to listen attentively to one's intuitive perceptions and not forcibly to disregard their warnings.*"

37

Much more could be said regarding this vast subject, but it is not possible in this lecture to go into further details. Rather I would like to focus on something particularly incisive: in various countries today laws allow pregnancy to be terminated during the first three months after conception. Even though not punishable under human law, this termination is not without consequences under the Laws of Creation. Let us examine why this is true.

The liveliest debates have taken place in connection with resolving the question about when human life actually begins. Some say at procreation and others say only at birth. Ultimately, without any compelling reasons, a time-limit of three months after conception was agreed upon.

Yet there is a very definite time in the course of human development when a fundamental change manifests clearly. It is when the expectant mother first distinctly feels the child's movements in her body. This point is about halfway through pregnancy and indicates that an incarnation has taken place. In other words, a human spirit has taken possession of the developing body.

Do you remember the description I gave you of the first coming-into-being of man on earth, and of how the most highly evolved animal body could continue its development into a human body only with the entry of the human spirit? In the conception and birth of every human being there is a reflection of that happening that once allowed mankind to emerge here on earth. Here at the midpoint of pregnancy—the developmental process, originally experienced in the material world—reaches its summit. The addition of the spirit is required to continue the development into a human being.

How does this entry of the spirit occur? Please recall what I said earlier about how radiation connects spirit, soul, and body. Not until the middle of pregnancy has the radiation of the developing body-covering attained sufficient strength to enable it to hold the spirit fast, with its finer coverings, that is to say the soul. It is radiation that draws the soul into the body. Only now can the spirit take possession of the developing body, make use of it, move it. If the concept "man" means this unified connection of spirit and body, we can then conclude that "earthman" begins to exist only at the moment of incarnation or in the middle of pregnancy.

But this does not mean that until then the developing body of the child may be treated arbitrarily or like an object. Although the spirit has not yet entered the body, connections between the two already exist. The incarnating spirit does not suddenly drop into the prepared body. The process is smooth, intensifying slowly, which explains why science is unable to define a discernible boundary here.

This process of incarnation of the spirit also refutes the widespread opinion that parents "give life" to their child. The spirit that is being embodied has long had life: it received it from its Creator. The parents can only "call" it into earthly existence if the spirit is still in need of an earth-life.

This call already begins with procreation. The union of egg and sperm results in a new blending of radiations that goes out like a transmitter frequency and is received by one tuned to the same frequency. We find the same principle in coarser form in technology involving a trans-

39

mitter and receiver. Today the ability to send signals to the Moon, Mars and Venus with very weak impulses, and to transmit commands to space probes, no longer surprises us. The call emitted by the new radiation-blending at procreation attracts the corresponding spirit whose inner relationship responds to the quality of the radiation. It is similar, on a much coarser plane, to the response elicited by the mating call of animals in nature.

In the Light of Truth describes this process very impressively:

"*You must know and understand that there are in the immediate beyond a great number of souls standing ready and awaiting the opportunity to reincarnate on earth. They are mostly human souls bound by threads of karma, which they are seeking to redeem in a new earth-life.*

"As soon as the possibility is presented, they attach themselves to where an act of procreation has taken place in order to await and follow up the growth of the new human body as a prospective dwelling. During this waiting period ethereal threads are spun from the young body to the soul—which keeps itself persistently in the immediate vicinity of the prospective mother—and from the soul to the young body. At a particular stage of maturity these threads serve as the bridge which permits the alien soul from the beyond to enter the young body and immediately take full possession."...

Perhaps now you can more easily imagine the significance of an intervention in this happening. Consider that everything which begins to form in the physical body must first have a finer prototype, an astral model. Thus any interference produces effects far beyond the body of the woman. Since such interference destroys the astral model before the entry of the spirit, it also tears the radiation threads that have formed between the waiting spirit and the developing body.

Surely in our earthly business life a factory owner would hardly think of destroying an article he was manufacturing in fulfillment of a promise to a customer on the basis of his proprietary right to the factory. At least he would realize that by such conduct he would violate the other person's interests and be liable for damages.

How then can we imagine that the termination of a pregnancy would not entail any responsibility? As I have said, the Fifth Commandment must not be interpreted materially. It embraces any kind of deadening—even that of hopes, talents and possibilities of development. With abortion, a human spirit's hopes for an earthlife offering redemption and spiritual advancement are destroyed, killed. Moreover, the parents thereby rob themselves of the possibility of karmic redemption, which in reality they cannot escape. It is merely postponed and only made more difficult by the fresh new entanglement.

It is never simply by chance that a spirit is incarnated with certain parents; there is a purpose behind it. Either a fateful entanglement, one from previous lives awaiting redemption, brings about such a connection, or the incarnation is determined by a fundamental Law of Creation, the Law of Attraction of Homogeneous Species, which likewise offers the parties concerned the opportunity to mature through each other.

I must say a few more things about this subject, because here too the ignorance of the spiritual has led to erroneous views. If a child has interests, talents and abilities already present in a parent, he is often said to have inherited these from his father or his mother—this is wrong. There is no heredity in the spiritual because each spirit is independent in itself and has traveled its own particular path of development. *His* experiences, *his* decisions and the reactions to them, have formed and brought him to the position he now occupies at the beginning of his new life.

The expression "birds of a feather flock together" refers to the Law of Attraction of Homogeneous Species, which brings together those who, as people say, "get on well" because they have similar inclinations. This "getting on well" is something non-physical. It concerns a spiritual homogeneity, meaning that these people "vibrate on the same wavelength." The social circle to which a person belongs, his many associations, are all based on this fact. "A man is known by the company he keeps" means that from this homogeneity we can even draw a conclusion about an individual's personality. Yet the people with whom he associates, meets in a club, are not related to him. Why then should we consider it heredity when such spiritual homogeneity occurs between parents and children? The proverb "like father, like son," frequently used in this connection, refers to nothing other than this Law of Attraction of Spiritually Homogeneous Species.

Therefore please keep in mind the decisive line of demarcation. Heredity exists only in the physical; in the spiritual there is the much more comprehensive Law of

Attraction of Homogeneous Species, which we wrongly regard as heredity because we know so little of the spirit. We can inherit blond hair, blue eyes, a birth-mark, or protruding ears—all pertaining to the material where the Mendelian Laws[3] apply—but never anything rooted in the condition of the spirit.

Certainly it is largely the spirit that forms the body. This explains physical similarities between parents and children, and often too between total strangers. You can observe that the qualities of a "double" are not restricted to external appearance only, but embrace the whole being: the style of conduct and speaking as well as interests. Here too it is not heredity but a homogeneity of spirit that fashions similar body forms.

This spiritual homogeneity also permits the incarnating spirit to find exactly those conditions that correspond to it, which because of its nature, it requires for its further spiritual development. For instance, a selfish, greedy man will be born in an atmosphere of greed and selfishness, where he will have to endure these same characteristics. In this lies not only justice, which permits him to experience what he formerly inflicted on others, but also helping love, which seeks to bring about insightful change through suffering induced by his own faults. In the same way a spirit that has already developed good qualities in previous lives finds an opportunity to advance and develop them further through the attraction of homogeneous species.

In the Light of Truth: The Grail Message states:

---

[3]The Mendelian Laws, from the research of Gregor Johann Mendel (1822-1884) are conclusions regarding the genetic inheritance of physical traits.

"This attraction power of all that is of the same nature, which is so important in the birth of a child, can proceed from the father, from the mother, or from anyone in the vicinity of the expectant mother. Therefore an expectant mother ought to be very careful whom she allows around her. *Consideration must be given to the fact that it is not in the outward character, but primarily in one's weaknesses that inner strength lies. Weaknesses bring important periods of inner experiencing that produce a strong power of attraction."*

This tells us something of enormous importance in two ways. Those aspects of our personality that still need improvement because they are not in accord with God's Laws, which we affectionately gloss over as "weaknesses" because we are not yet strong enough to confront our wrong desires successfully, are exactly those aspects that can be decisive in the attraction of homogeneous species. Our surrender to these weaknesses and the resulting inner struggle have led to particularly strong experiences.

The above quote also says that the *surroundings* of the mother can play an important part in the process. An alien radiation, brought about by the parents' lack of care, can disturb the lawful course of events as if the parent's own frequency had been "jammed." This interference explains why occasionally a "black sheep" can enter an otherwise good family.

All this clarifies the great spiritual responsibility parents have in the conception and birth of a human being. Provided that fateful entanglements have not occurred, parents can exercise a degree of choice from among the human spirits awaiting an incarnation by their spiritual attitude and attention to their surroundings and therefore protect themselves from a guest who may be less than agreeable.

Having learned of the Law of Attraction of Homogeneous Species, you will, upon reflection, also perceive what would seem to be a contradiction. Do we not also say, "Opposites attract one another?" And can we not find this axiom manifested in the world? Which principle, then, holds true? Let me discuss this apparent contradiction, since both statements are correct. Here *In the Light of Truth* offers an explanation: wherever there is a division into polarities such as plus-minus, active-passive, or male-female, these opposites attract each other because such *split* species desire to reconnect in a complementary way. To the species *complete* in themselves however, the Law of Attraction of Homogeneous Species applies. Humanity, for example, is split into men and women. Between them is the desire for union that characterizes a split species. On the other hand qualities such as self-seeking, avarice, the love of Nature, musicality and countless others—in short all human inclinations, interests and abilities—are species complete in themselves and attract their homogeneous species.

To what abnormalities ignorance of these hidden connections gives rise has been clearly demonstrated recently in cases of "surrogate mothers." I refer particularly to a couple who, unable to have children in the natural way, allow the egg to be fertilized in a test-tube, and then implanted and carried until birth by another woman. In such a manner, the coming-into-being of a human being is debased to a functional, matter-of-course production process—in the legal sense a kind of work contract. A child is "manufactured" from material made available for the purpose. Those who imagine that they can acquire a child "of their own" by this roundabout method proceed under a delusion. The child may outwardly exhibit similarities to the parents, but the spirit within, which is after all the actual human being, will bring with it qualities, weaknesses, and tendencies similar to those in the "surrogate mother" or those around her.

These hidden connections also explain the increasing decline of our world, including the growth in crime and violence. Just consider our indifference about the very important event of human conception and our ignorance of the spiritual responsibility involved, our carelessness about the company we keep, our fascination with crime and immorality purely for the pleasure of sensation (just think of movies, television and the press), and finally our materialistic lifestyle. All these can only lead to ever more spirits reaching the earth who bring from previous lives a lack of moral responsibility and greed for material things.

Lacking knowledge of the actual causes that lie in the spiritual, people easily tend to assume that the Creator is responsible for the deplorable state of our modern world. They feel there is no justice and think there is a blind senselessness in the distribution of births, whose inequality must be leveled as far as possible with social legislation. Yet one sentence from *In the Light of Truth*, combined with the knowledge of rebirth, could solve all these problems:

46

"*The inequality among men is only the inevitable consequence of their own free will, of their voluntary decisions from former lives!*"

In the workings of the immutable Laws of God there is no injustice. Just as a key proves useful only for the lock that it fits—because only there can it work in its own way—so an incarnating spirit is placed into those conditions that offer the appropriate possibilities for *its* development. But in the example thus presented we see the analogy with the parental responsibility mentioned earlier: it is the lock that determines which key will fit.

The environment into which we are born is, so to speak, the launching pad that we ourselves have prepared from the sum total of our previous lives for our ongoing life-journey. We ourselves determine where this journey is to lead, for we can redeem all fateful entanglements through our firm volition for the good and for spiritual ascent. That indeed is the wonderful comfort inherent in this lawfulness. Unfortunately I cannot enter into this more fully in this lecture. But help upon help is available to us if only we finally learn to make use of the furthering effect of these laws by gaining understanding of them. After all, many inventions of which we are proud are based on their utilization. With an understanding of the Laws we can now begin to answer life's questions; but without this knowledge we have faced these questions helplessly and uneasily, making decisions based an an erroneous concept of "right and wrong." Even the experts concede, as I stated earlier, "but of man we know nothing."

Therefore we cannot expect any clarification from them. Let us then look to the words of *In the Light of Truth* for clarification:

> "*B ut how foolish you are, you men, how narrowly you have constricted your outlook on everything, particularly on that which concerns you and your wanderings through the Creations.*"

Let us at last burst the narrow limitations of our field of vision! Let us follow the instruction of *In the Light of Truth:*

> "*B ecome spiritual at last, you men, for you are of the spirit!*"

I hope you will have observed that throughout these reflections I have not in any way altered the well-known facts and findings established by science. I have only included the spiritual, which has been disregarded until now. And suddenly those facts that stood alone, leaving numerous unsolved questions, begin to make sense.

While the range has been limited, I have offered you an array of topics that certainly concern all human beings and that especially have filled our minds in recent years. Much more could be said since I have only discussed the topic of "Why Was I Born?" in broad outline. Even so, much may have sounded new, unfamiliar or perhaps even strange to you. Free yourselves from rigid, encrusted thought patterns! In our time we are faced again and again with the necessity to rethink many opinions. Fresh insights will show you the way.

As the American physicist Gary Zukav said, "The new world-vision calls upon us to abandon many of our deep-rooted world-views, our firmly-held ideas." This statement refers not only to natural science but to all aspects of life. Increasingly we must learn to fit our splintered, fragmented recognitions into a great, comprehensive order. We are being forced to think holistically. This type of thinking is no longer satisfied with outward appearances, but must include the interweaving at work behind the appearances. Such demands apply all the more to our humanity and purpose of existence, from which the decisive factor—the spirit and its development—can no longer be excluded. Nothing more is demanded of you but to step across the obstruction erected by skepticism that prevents so many of us from recognizing ourselves as spiritual beings and our existence as a vast, purposeful whole.

If you are ready for such a comprehensive expansion of your worldview, if you are a human being who honestly seeks the Truth, then I refer you to the book I have repeatedly mentioned, *In the Light of Truth: The Grail Message* by Abd-ru-shin (Grail Foundation Press, 1995). For it is not I who have presumed to enlighten you about humanity's problems. Only the manner in which I have tried to present them, the bridges I have built for you, stem from me. If you think I have sometimes oversimplified things by using examples from everyday events, you are quite right! For everything great and true is simple, and this simplicity entails our rediscovering this truth everywhere.

First, however, our eyes must be open to it. This is the invaluable merit of the one who wrote this work and explained in it the Laws of Creation and our path in Creation. The obvious question of the source of this knowledge is answered in the book itself.

However, everything introduced to you here must be reflected upon carefully. We learn from the author of *In the Light of Truth* that one should not simply adopt the opinions and assertions of others. Rather, he wants the conviction of the rightness of the work to grow out of yourselves. As he writes in the foreword to *In the Light of Truth:*

"*Conviction comes solely through an inflexible weighing and examining!*"

In conclusion, one more clarification is called for so that you do not misunderstand me. In our modern age, so contaminated with commercialism, a certain distrust is unfortunately not out of place. My purpose is solely to offer you help—help in solving the problems of your life, help in the search for God, so often beset with many doubts, and help in finding an answer to the ultimately decisive question of whether or not HE really exists.

If you have received a little of *that* help from my words and above all from the words of *In the Light of Truth*, I shall be happy. The author of *In the Light of Truth* has expressed this aim in words with which I wish to close my remarks, since, to my mind, I can add nothing to them:

"*In order to convey to mankind such knowledge, which gives them a clear and intelligible conviction of the working of God in His Justice and Love, I have written the Work 'In the Light of Truth,' which leaves no gap, contains the answer to every question, and clearly shows mankind how wonderful are the ways in Creation that are upheld by many servants of His Will.*

"Not a single question remains unsolved for you; a great understanding arises within you of the mysterious working of the adamantine Laws in Creation, which guide you with the outworkings of your volition; and as a crowning for your trouble comes the wonderful divining of a Wisdom, of an Omnipotence, of a Love and of a Justice that can only issue from God, Whose Being you therewith discover!"

If you have questions about the content of this lecture,
please contact Reader Services at:

Grail Foundation Press
P. O. Box 45
Gambier, Ohio 43022
Telephone: 614.427-9410
Fax: 614.427-4954

Abd-ru-shin. In the Light of Truth: The Grail Message. Gambier, Ohio: Grail Foundation Press, 1995.

Ditfurth, Hoimar von. Wir sind nicht nur von dieser Welt. München: Deutscher Taschenbuch Verlag, 1987.

Eigen, Manfred. Stufen zum Leben. München: Piper, 1987.

Goethe, Johann Wolfgang von. Torquato Tasso. Munchen: Deutscher Taschenbuch Verlag, 1967.

Koestler, Arthur. Der Mensch: Irrläufer der Evolution. Bern/München:Scherz Verlag, 1978.

Popper, Karl R. and John C. Eccles. The Self and Its Brain. New York: Springer International, 1977.

Steinpach, Richard. Why We Live After Death. Gambier, Ohio: Grail Foundation Press, 1995.

Vester, Frederic. Neuland des Denkens. Stuttgart: Deutsche Verlags-Anstalt, 1980.

Zukav, Gary. The Dancing Wu Li Masters: An Overview of the New Physics. New York: Morrow, 1979.

*D**r. Richard Steinpach** was born in Vienna in 1917 where he was a lawyer for forty years. His professional life provided extensive opportunities to observe human nature, and to deal with many life-questions and problems. Between 1979 and 1991, he gave hundreds of lectures throughout Germany, Austria, and Switzerland. The powerful response of his audiences convinced him to publish his manuscripts in book form. Dr. Steinpach died in 1992.*

In The Light Of Truth: The Grail Message
An Introduction

....

*I*N THE LIGHT OF TRUTH: THE GRAIL MESSAGE
*is a classic work that offers clear and perceptive
answers to questions which challenge every human
being. Written between the years 1923-1938, it is
a collection of 168 lectures addressing all spheres of
life ranging from life after death to God and the Universe,
the Laws in Creation, free will, intuition and the intellect,
the ethereal world and the beyond, justice and love. It
answers eternal questions such as what does it mean to be
human, what is the purpose of life on earth, and what happens to "me" when I die.* In the Light of Truth: The Grail
Message *explains the causes and significance of the unprecedented crises facing humanity, and our responsibilities to the
future.*

*The author, Abd-ru-shin, was born in 1875 in Bischof-
swerda, Germany. His given name was Oskar Ernst Bernhardt. After being educated and trained in business, he
established himself in Dresden and became financially successful. In the years that followed, he made many journeys
abroad, and wrote successful travel books, stories and plays.*

*After residing for some time in New York, Mr. Bernhardt
journeyed to England, and in 1913, moved to London.*

There, the outbreak of World War I took him unawares, and in 1914 he was interned on the Isle of Man.

The seclusion of internment brought with it an inner deepening. He reflected continuously over questions connected with the meaning of life, birth and death, responsibility and free will, and with God and Creation. More and more the desire awakened within him to help humanity. He was released in the Spring of 1919 and returned to Germany.

In the 1920s, Abd-ru-shin gave public lectures. His explanation of the Knowledge of Creation resounded among his hearers. He began to write the first lectures for In the Light of Truth: The Grail Message *in 1923.*

In 1928, Abd-ru-shin settled in Austria on a mountain plateau called Vomperberg, where he continued writing The Grail Message. *The seizure of power in Austria by the Nazis in 1938 ended his work there. On March 12 of that year he was arrested, and his land and property were appropriated without compensation. In September, he was placed under house arrest, first in Schlauroth near Görlitz, and later in Kipsdorf in the Erzgebirge, where he was constantly under surveillance by the Gestapo. He was forbidden any further work for making* The Grail Message *known publicly.*

On December 6, 1941, Abd-ru-shin died from the effects of these measures.

In 1991, upon the fiftieth anniversary of his death, the Dresdner Nachrichten *newspaper published an article that included:*

"THE GRAIL MESSAGE, which Oskar Ernst Bernhardt began to write in 1923 in Dresden, has now been translated

into almost all the civilized languages of the western hemi-sphere, and is available ... around the globe. It was forbidden in the 'Third Reich,' but was also on the list of banned literature in East Germany. These periods of prohibition (in East Germany more than fifty years) markedly curtailed the possibility of disseminating The Grail Message *and making it known. One wonders why a non-political book like* The Grail Message *was still regarded by political systems as a 'source of danger.' The reason, perhaps, is that it sets up personal awareness of responsibility and individual freedom of choice against all conformity. Furthermore dogmatic limitations are alien to it, since it gives a comprehensive understanding, on the basis of the Laws of Creation, of the world and of life—beyond nationalities, races, and creeds."*

Concerning In the Light of Truth: The Grail Message, *Abd-ru-shin writes:*

> "I wish to fill the gaps which so far have remained unanswered in the souls of men as burning questions, and which never leave any serious thinker in peace."

Throughout The Grail Message *readers are urged to weigh questions and answers intuitively, to confront them within their own life experiences, and only to believe that which they can perceive inwardly. Only through this process can one reach true conviction in one's life.*

What follows is an abstract introducing some of the many principles contained in The Grail Message. *Full explanations are given within the work itself, and the brief discussion below can in no way substitute for the original.*

61

In the Light of Truth: The Grail Message *explains that human spirits emanated from the spiritual domain at the summit of Creation. God created the universe, and man is a part of that Creation. As such, God stands above Creation and man's place is within Creation. Creation has many different visible and invisible spheres of activity and substance. The meaning of human life on Earth and in the beyond is to develop spiritually so as to return to our primordial origin as fully conscious spirits.*

When a spirit comes to the material world for the first time in order to mature, it begins to make conscious choices for itself. Choices that do not swing with God's Laws burden the spirit with responsibility to redeem these choices either in the present lifetime, or in the spirit's subsequent reincarnations. Reincarnations provide spirits with direct opportunities to redeem the obligations they have created and to develop towards maturity.

God's Laws govern all of Creation, and, since human beings stand within Creation, these laws operate upon them whether or not they acknowledge this fact. Everything in Creation, without exception, is interconnected. Every circumstance in life is a result of the choices a spirit makes, and every circumstance is an opportunity to mature.

The Law of Motion: only with motion (vibrations) can there be life, and only with continual striving for ennoblement can there be ascent toward spiritual maturity. The higher one ascends, the faster and lighter are one's vibrations. The lower one descends, the slower and heavier are one's vibrations.

The Law of Gravity: everything that is noble, beautiful, pure or light produces an uplifting effect, while everything base, ignoble, or impure produces a sinking, dragging down effect. Therefore, after leaving this earth, every human being will enter that sphere that accords with its density. The Law of Gravity, combined with the Law of Attraction of Homogeneous Species, compels those of similar nature to be together.

The Law of Attraction of Homogeneous Species: like attracts like. Whatever emanates from a soul produces vibrations that take on forms corresponding exactly with their nature. Like forms attract each other, creating power centers that affect human beings according to their nature. When combined with the Law of Reciprocal Action, a single thought or action sent out returns strengthened by the Law of Attraction of Homogeneous Species.

The Law of Reciprocal Action: individuals reap what they sow; whatever emanates returns. Therefore, we are responsible for our every action and thought. If the action or thought is positive, then we ennoble Creation, and contribute to the advancement of the human race. If our actions or thoughts are negative, they bind us to whoever and whatever we harm, creating a karma that must be redeemed.

Individuals have free will. Each can decide whether or not to swing with the Laws in Creation, but the effects react upon them in either case. Human beings stand within Creation, and are responsible for their free choices. Man can only progress through an understanding of and adherence to these Laws.

Man's greatest error has been to place himself above God's Will. This arrogance has caused people to go forth blindly with destructive behavior, with thoughts and actions contrary to God's Will, thereby retarding their development toward spiritual maturity. The tool that human beings have most often misused is their intellect. They have overdeveloped the intellect at the cost of their intuition, their true spiritual connection. Indolence of spirit is a great weakness for many people, and the root cause of many of life's problems. This indolence has, over time, caused humans' spiritual abilities to become stunted through lack of use and has allowed the emergence of "intellectual mankind."

Within Creation, a multitude of helpers is available to us. Through the Laws of Creation, if an individual emanates pure thoughts and actions, they return strengthened and uplifted by similar thoughts and actions. We attract homogeneous species even more quickly and strongly from the unseen world. Everyone has guides, but most people have cut themselves off from these helps through the overdevelopment of their intellect and negligence of their intuition. Humans must learn to live harmoniously with each other and within Creation: this includes the world of nature.

Everything in Creation works in cycles (the Law of Motion). According to their nature, all cycles must end where they began. Human beings do not have unlimited opportunities for reincarnation in order to redeem karma and ascend spiritually. Only by swinging fully with God's Laws will we be able to continue our existence within Creation.

God's Justice, as seen in His constant, unvarying Laws, and His creation of humans in the first place, allowing us to live joyously in Creation and to ennoble that which is around us, gives evidence of His great Love.

In the Light of Truth: The Grail Message *is directed solely to the individual human being, irrespective of creed, nationality or race. It gives comprehensive explanations of the laws that govern the universe including the visible, material world and the various spheres through which the human spirit journeys on its return to its primordial origin. A work which will bring disquiet into many circles, its tone is uplifting, but severe. It requires that each individual is fully responsible for every action and thought produced, whether one accepts that responsibility or not.*

Other Titles from Grail Foundation Press

IN THE LIGHT OF TRUTH: THE GRAIL MESSAGE
•
THE TEN COMMANDMENTS OF GOD
THE LORD'S PRAYER
•
LAO-TSE
•
BUDDHA
•
ZOROASTER
•
WHY WE LIVE AFTER DEATH
•
HOW CAN GOD ALLOW SUCH THINGS?
•

available at your local bookstore
or directly through the publisher

GRAIL PUBLICATIONS
◊ ◊ ◊
P.O. Box 412, Chénéville, Qc. J0V 1E0
Tel / Fax: 1 (800) 672-2898

Publisher's catalog available on request

IN THE LIGHT OF TRUTH: THE GRAIL MESSAGE
by Abd-ru-shin

In the Light of Truth: The Grail Message is a classic work that offers clear and perceptive answers to questions which challenge every human being. This collection of 168 essays addresses all spheres of life ranging from God and the Universe to the Laws in Creation, the meaning of life, responsibility, free will, intuition and the intellect, the ethereal world and the beyond, justice and love. *The Grail Message* will appeal to any human being who is seeking to understand life, his or her place in Creation, and the source of one's being.

Linen edition, three volumes combined
ISBN 1-57461-006-6
5.5" x 8.5"
1,062 pages
Paper edition, three-volume boxed set
ISBN 1-57461-003-1
6" x 9"
1,079 pages

Original edition: German
Translations available in:
Czech, Dutch, English, Estonian, French, Hungarian,
Italian, Portuguese, Rumanian, Russian,
Slovak, Spanish

THE TEN COMMANDMENTS OF GOD
THE LORD'S PRAYER
by Abd-ru-shin

Clearly explained in their full, life-embracing meaning, *The Ten Commandments of God and The Lord's Prayer* is a book for anyone striving to live with integrity. Readers who bring these Commandments to life within themselves will find they create a solid foundation for their daily lives and for their existence beyond physical death. Abd-ru-shin's insights regarding the Lord's Prayer help the reader understand this "key to the Kingdom of God" in its profound significance for mankind.

Linen edition
ISBN 1-57461-007-4
5" x 7.5"
72 pages
Paper edition
ISBN 1-57461-004-X
5" x 7.5"
72 pages

Original edition: German
Translations available in:
Czech, Dutch, English, French, Italian, Portuguese,
Russian, Slovak, Spanish

LAO-TSE
*The Life and Work
of the Forerunner in China*

Little is known about the life and work of this enlightened Chinese sage. In *Lao-Tse*, the personality of this leader and the events of his life are simply and clearly portrayed. The first in a series, this wonderful story was transcribed from the direct experience of living pictures taken from the Book of Life by one gifted to do so.

*Paper edition
ISBN 1-57461-008-2
6" x 9"
288 Pages*

*Original Edition: German
Translations available in:
Czech, English, French*

BUDDHA
*The Life and Work
of the Forerunner in India*

With beauty and grace, this book creates the images of the life of Buddha so that when reading it, one experiences his life as if in living pictures. The story unfolds naturally and is easy and compelling to read. Buddha's relationship to God is clearly defined, and it reveals both the events of his outward life and his inner spiritual development.

The reader sees how Buddha was helped by the events of his life, many of which seemed on the surface to be great misfortune. However, it was through overcoming suffering that Buddha came to the recognition of his purpose in life. His misfortune turned into his greatest help. As a sage of the Word of Truth, he worked in the midst of his people, whom he wished to lead away from a life that submitted indolently to fate to one activated by conviction.

*Paper edition
ISBN 1-57461-010-4
6" x 9"
278 Pages*

*Original Edition: German
Translations available in:
Czech, English, French*

ZOROASTER
The Life and Work
of the Forerunner in Persia

In ancient Persia, the prophet Zoroaster brought to his people a way of life that united them for 1000 years, and made the land now known as Iran into a fertile, prosperous region. Known by Plato, Aristotle, and other Greek thinkers, Zoroaster's teachings helped shape the development of Judeo-Christian thought and have been preserved in the sacred scripture known as the Avesta.

Zoroaster: Life and Work of the Forerunner in Persia is the first general-audience biography of the great Persian sage. As the long-awaited herald, Zoroaster, it was his purpose to unite the people of Persia into a belief of one God, Ahuramazda, and to announce the coming of the Son of Man, the Saoshyant, who would lead this world into and through the Last Judgement. Before Zoroaster's arrival, the land of Persia was consumed by natural disasters that destroyed most of the people and almost all of their structures. A new society had to be built literally from the ground up, this time based upon God's Laws, rather than man's.

Although *Zoroaster: Life and Work of the Forerunner in Persia* is a book drawn from the past, it is particularly relevant for today.

Paper edition
ISBN 1-57461-012-0
6" x 9"
264 Pages

Original Edition: German
Translations available in:
Czech, English, French

WHY WE LIVE AFTER DEATH
by Dr. Richard Steinpach

Accounts of people who had clinically "died" and then been brought back to life are no longer considered fantasy: they have been scientifically proven. However, most writings about life after death have simply reported such accounts and supplied statistical data. Richard Steinpach's work goes much further: by applying Laws of Creation, he explains how we continue to develop after physical death. *Why We Live After Death* opens the door to a fuller understanding of the totality of our existence, and makes it possible for readers to answer the eternal question, "What is the meaning of life?"

Paper edition
ISBN 1-57461-005-8
6" x 9"
96 Pages

Original Edition: German
Translations available in:
Czech, Dutch, English, French, Hungarian, Italian,
Portuguese, Roumanian, Russian, Slovak, Spanish

over 500,000 copies printed

HOW CAN GOD ALLOW SUCH THINGS?
by Dr. Richard Steinpach

Human suffering is both universal and unavoidable. Even if it is not currently present in our own lives, we are reminded of it daily through the media. Accounts of people who have had to deal with serious tragedies and handicaps are well-known. However, most explain such occurrences as "God's will," destiny or mystery. Dr. Steinpach gives logical explanations for the hardships we face. He applies the universal Laws in Creation to our life on earth and in the beyond, and offers a radical perspective concerning personal responsibility.

How Can God Allow Such Things? opens the door to a fuller understanding of the totality of our existence, and makes it possible for readers to answer the eternal question, "Why me?"

Paper edition
ISBN 1-57461-009-0
6" x 9"
96 Pages

Original Edition: German
Translations available in:
Czech, Dutch, English, French, Hungarian, Italian,
Portuguese, Rumanian, Russian, Slovak, Spanish

Over 100,000 copies printed